# ◢ LIVING ON THE EDGE™

# FREE ACCESS TO VIDEO TEACHING

You can stream it for FREE by following the directions below.
Or you can order a DVD at (888) 333-6003 or
LivingontheEdge.org.

## YOUR ONLINE CODE

# 7441045-47SH-WCDQ

 Please visit LivingontheEdge.org/access and enter this code.

## 3 EASY STEPS

**1** | **CREATE AN ACCOUNT**
Go to LivingontheEdge.org/access and complete
the steps to create your FREE account.

**2** | **GET IMMEDIATE ACCESS**
Now you will be connected to the resources which
will be needed throughout this workbook.

**3** | **ACCESS ANYTIME**
- Log back into your account anytime by visiting
LivingontheEdge.org and click on STORE.
- From the STORE page, click on Login/Register.
- Enter your login information. Once you are in your
account, click on MEMBERSHIPS.

D1016485

Transformed

LIVING ON THE EDGE
BIBLE STUDY

# TRANS*formed*

## The Miracle of Life Change

# CHIPINGRAM

**TRANS**_formed_  The Miracle of Life Change

# Table of Contents

## How to Start Your Own Small Group

The fact that you are even reading this page says a lot about you. It says that you are either one of those people who has to read everything, or it says you are open to God using you to lead a group.

Leading a small group can sound intimidating, but it really doesn't have to be. Think of it more as gathering a few friends to get to know each other better and to have some discussion around spiritual matters.

Here are a few practical tips to help you get started:

1.  **Pray** – One of the most important principles of spiritual leadership is to realize you can't do this on your own. No matter how long you've been a christian or been involved in ministry, you need the power of the Holy Spirit. Lean on Him…He will help you.

2.  **Invite some friends** – Don't be afraid to ask people to come to your group. You will be surprised how many people are open to a study like this. Whether you have four or 14 in your group, it can be a powerful experience. You should probably plan on at least an hour and a half for your group meeting.

3.  **Get your materials** – Included with your study guide is a personal streaming code that you can use to view the video teaching by Chip Ingram. DVDs are available at livingontheedge.org. It is helpful for each person to have their own study guide; additional study guides can be purchased through the website.

4.  **Watch the coaching videos** – We have put together a brief video for each session that will give you a couple of tips about facilitating that week's study. Log onto livingontheedge.org/cultureshockcoaching.

5.  **Be prepared to facilitate** – Just a few minutes a week in preparation can make a huge difference in the group experience. Each week, preview the video teaching and review the discussion questions. If you don't think your group can get through all the questions, select the ones that are most relevant to your group.

6.  **Learn to say "I don't know"** – This series takes on some of the most difficult questions that Christians and non-Christians struggle with. These sessions will spark some lively and spirited discussions. When tough questions come up, it's ok for you to say, "I don't know." Take the pressure off. No one expects you to have all the answers.

7.  **Love your group** – Maybe the most important thing you bring to the group is your personal care for them. If you will pray for them, encourage them, call them, e-mail them, involve them, and love them, God will be pleased and you will have a very meaningful experience.

Thank you for your availability. May God bless you as you serve Him by serving others.

# How to Get the Most Out of This Experience

You are about to begin a powerful journey exploring some of the most controversial issues of our generation. This powerful series taught by Chip Ingram provides in-depth teaching as well as challenging, practical application.

Below, you will find a list of each week's segments as well as some hints for getting the most out of this experience. If you are leading the group, you will find some additional help and coaching on page 119.

1.   Take It In (Watch the Video)

It is important for us to get before God and submit ourselves to His truth. During this section you will watch the video teaching by Chip. He will introduce each session with a personal word to the group followed by the teaching portion of the video. At the end of the teaching segment, Chip will wrap up the session and help the group dive into discussion.

A teaching outline with fill-ins is provided for each session. As you follow along, write down questions or insights that you can share during the discussion time.

Even though most of the verses will appear on the screen and in your notes, it is a great idea to bring your own Bible each week. It will allow you to make notes in your own Bible and find other passages that might be relevant to that week's study.

2.   Talk It Over

We not only grow by listening to God's word, but we grow in community. The friendship and insights of those in the group will enrich your small group experience. Several discussion questions are provided for your group to further engage the teaching content. Keep the following guidelines in mind for having a healthy group discussion.

- **Be involved.** Jump in and share your thoughts. Your ideas are important and you have a perspective that is unique and can benefit the other group members.

- **Be a good listener.** Value what others are sharing. Seek to really understand the perspective of others in your group and don't be afraid to ask follow up questions.

- **Be courteous.** People hold strong opinions about the topics in this study. Spirited discussion is great. Disrespect and attack is not. When there is disagreement, focus on the issue and never turn the discussion into a personal attack.

- **Be focused.** Stay on topic. Help the group explore the subject at hand and try to save unrelated questions or stories for afterwards.

- **Be careful not to dominate.** Be aware of the amount of talking you are doing in proportion to the rest of the group and make space for others to speak.

- **Be a learner.** Stay sensitive to what God might be wanting to teach you through the lesson, as well as through what others have to say. Focus more on your own growth rather than making a point or winning an argument.

3.  Live It Out — B.I.O.
    The word "bio" means "life". Found in those three simple letters B.I.O. is the key to
    helping you become the person God wants you to be.

    **B = Come "Before God" Daily**
    Meet with Him personally through His word and prayer to enjoy His presence, receive
    His direction, and follow His will

    **I = Do Life "In Community" Weekly**
    Structure your week to personally connect in safe relationships that provide love,
    support, transparency, challenge, and accountability

    **O = Be "On Mission" 24/7**
    Cultivate a mindset to "live out" Jesus' love for others through acts of sacrifice and
    service at home, work, play, and church.

4.  Accelerate (20 minutes that turn concepts into convictions)

    ***Inspiration*** comes from hearing God's Word; ***Motivation*** grows by discussing God's
    Word; ***Transformation*** occurs when you study it for yourself.

    If you want to "accelerate" your growth, here is an assignment you can do at home each
    week. Our convictions become even stronger when we dig into scripture and discover
    truth for ourselves. To help you get the most out of this exercise, consider partnering
    up with somebody in your group who will also commit to do the assignment this week.
    Then, after you have each done the assignment, agree to spend 10 minutes by phone to
    share what you learned and what you are applying.

# Is a "Changed Life" Really Possible?

## Part 1

**TRANS*formed***

The Miracle of Life Change

## Introduction: A Picture, A Problem, and A Process

- The Picture - Metamorphosis

- The Problem - Why do we long to change, grow, improve and be transformed; yet find it so difficult?

- The Process - Spiritual metamorphosis

## What does spiritual metamorphosis look like in real life?

1. **Spiritual Birth** = _____ - Jesus gives me new life.
   ROMANS 5:1

2. **Spiritual Growth** = _____ - Jesus changes me to be progressively more like Him.
   2 CORINTHIANS 5:17

3. **Spiritual Maturity** = _____ - Jesus changes me forever when I see Him face to face.
   1 JOHN 3:2

**Is Morphing for everyone?**

*And do not be conformed to this world, but be transformed by the renewing of your mind, so that you may prove what the will of God is, that which is good and acceptable and perfect.*

**ROMANS 12:2**

# HOW GOD TRANSFORMS HIS CHILDREN

**The Call** - Let Jesus Live His Life Through You

*As a prisoner for the Lord, then, I urge you to live a life worthy of the calling you have received.*

**EPHESIANS 4:1 (NIV)**

## Talk It Over

1. Think back to the church you grew up in, or those early days after you became a Christian. What did it look like to be a "good Christian"? And, if you could summarize what you were taught about living the Christian life, what would you say?

   ------------------------------------------------------------

   ------------------------------------------------------------

   ------------------------------------------------------------

2.  What are a couple of ways in which your life has been transformed (morphed) by knowing Christ?

-----------------------------------------------------------

-----------------------------------------------------------

-----------------------------------------------------------

3.  Describe a season in your life when you were experiencing spiritual growth? What were you doing or what was happening that was causing the growth?

-----------------------------------------------------------

-----------------------------------------------------------

-----------------------------------------------------------

4.  What's the one thing you would really like for God to change in your life?

-----------------------------------------------------------

-----------------------------------------------------------

-----------------------------------------------------------

## Live It Out — B.I.O.

BIO is a word that is synonymous with "life". Found in those 3 simple letters B.I.O. is the key to helping you become the person God wants you to be.

**B = Come Before God Daily**
To meet with Him personally through His word and prayer to enjoy His presence, receive His direction, and follow His will

**I = Do Life in Community Weekly**
Structuring your week to personally connect in safe relationships that provide love, support, transparency, challenge, and accountability

**O = Be on Mission 24/7**
Cultivating a mindset to "live out" Jesus' love for others through acts of sacrifice and service at home, work, play, and church

**Come Before God**

5. Many Christians live defeated lives because their view of the Christian life is performance based (do good, try hard, keep the rules). What changes when you view the Christian life more relationally?

_____

_____

_____

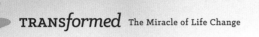 

**Do Life in Community**

6.  In the "morphing" or life-change process, why do you think it is important to be in authentic community with other believers? What steps could you and your group take to deepen the level of authentic community?

    _____

    _____

    _____

**Be on Mission**

7.  In Ephesians 4:1, Paul challenges us to live a life "worthy of the calling you have received." Who is somebody that you know that is living a life "worthy" of their calling? What sets their life apart?

    _____

    _____

    _____

## Accelerate (20 minutes that turns concepts into convictions)

*Inspiration* comes from hearing God's Word; ***Motivation*** grows by discussing God's Word; ***Transformation*** occurs when you study it for yourself.

If you want to "accelerate" your growth, here is an assignment you can do this week. To help you get the most out of this exercise, consider partnering up with somebody in your group who will also commit to do the assignment this week. Then, after you have each done the assignment, agree to spend 10 minutes by phone to share what you learned and what you are applying.

**Come Before God**

1.  Read the following passage carefully and slowly. Go to youversion.com where you can find several other translations of this passage.

    *As a prisoner for the Lord, then, I urge you to live a life worthy of the calling you have received. Be completely humble and gentle; be patient, bearing with one another in love. Make every effort to keep the unity of the Spirit through the bond of peace.*

    **EPHESIANS 4:1-3 (NIV)**

2.  In verse 1, Paul talks about living a life worthy of the "calling you have received". Go back and read Ephesians 1:3-14 to get a picture of the spiritual blessings we have in Christ. From this passage, make a list of all of the spiritual blessings that are yours in Christ Jesus.

    _____

    _____

    _____

3.  Reflect on Paul's command for us to live a life worthy of the calling we have received. Write out a handful of statements that would further define what it looks like for you to live a worthy life.

    _____

    _____

    _____

4.  As you come before God this week, go back to the question that was asked in your group discussion. What is it that you would really like for God to change in your life? Linger over this question. Now write out a prayer expressing your longing to God.

------------------------------------------------------------

------------------------------------------------------------

------------------------------------------------------------

### Do Life In Community

5.  Get together with a Christian friend this week. Then, take some time for each of you to share the story of your faith journey. Share not only how you came to faith in Christ, but also how God has been morphing (changing) you along the way.

### Be On Mission

6.  How would living a "worthy" life help you in sharing your faith with those around you?

------------------------------------------------------------

------------------------------------------------------------

------------------------------------------------------------

Session 2

# Is a "Changed Life" Really Possible?

Part 2

## TRANS*formed*
The Miracle of Life Change

# HOW GOD TRANSFORMS HIS CHILDREN

**The Call** - Let Jesus Live His Life Through You

*As a prisoner for the Lord, then, I urge you to live a life worthy of the calling you have received.*

EPHESIANS 4:1 (NIV)

**The Process** - Practice Sacrificial, Other-Centered Relationships

*Be completely humble and gentle; be patient, bearing with one another in love. Make every effort to keep the unity of the Spirit through the bond of peace.*

EPHESIANS 4:2-3 (NIV)

**The Reason** – Christ's Church Must Reflect His Character

*There is one body and one Spirit—just as you were called to one hope when you were called—one Lord, one faith, one baptism; one God and Father of all, who is over all and through all and in all.*

EPHESIANS 4:4-6 (NIV)

**Three Reasons We Fail to Be Transformed:**

1.  Spiritual _____.

    Our failure to understand our true identity in Christ destines us to the "try hard - do good - failure" syndrome.

    *   The Problem = Lack of _____.

    *   The Solution = _____ your new identity.

                                                        GALATIANS 2:20

2.  Spiritual _____ .

    Our failure to actively participate in deep, Christ-centered, honest relationships, makes transformation impossible.

    *   The Problem = _____ .

    *   The Solution = Do life in _____ .

                                                        HEBREWS 3:13

3.  Spiritual _____ .

    Our failure to grasp what's really at stake when Christians don't live like Christians minimizes our motivation and destroys our testimony.

    *   The Problem = Our Culture of _____ .

    *   The Solution = Get a High Holy View of _____.

                                                        ROMANS 11:33-36

## Talk It Over

1. Where did you get your current view of God? How has our consumer culture impacted people's view of God and the Christian life?

   ------------------------------------------------

   ------------------------------------------------

   ------------------------------------------------

2. Of the 4 attitudes that Chip discussed (humility, gentleness, patience, and bearing with one another), which one do you most need to work on? How can this group support you as you seek to live out that attitude?

   ------------------------------------------------

   ------------------------------------------------

   ------------------------------------------------

3. When it comes to the church, what is the difference between "unity" and "uniformity"?

   ------------------------------------------------

   ------------------------------------------------

   ------------------------------------------------

4.  Chip said there are three reasons we fail to morph – Spiritual ignorance, isolation, and myopia. Which of these three reasons do you most need to pay attention to? Why?

------------------------------------------------

------------------------------------------------

------------------------------------------------

## Live It Out — B.I.O.

### Come Before God

5.  Chip said the solution to spiritual myopia is getting a high and holy view of God. Honestly, how are you doing at consistently coming before God and spending time in Scripture? What adjustments could you make to spend more time in God's Word?

------------------------------------------------

------------------------------------------------

------------------------------------------------

### Do Life In Community

6.  Failure to participate in honest, real, and authentic relationships is a major barrier to spiritual transformation. What is the biggest roadblock to you experiencing deeper, authentic community?

------------------------------------------------

------------------------------------------------

------------------------------------------------

**Be On Mission**

7. Where do you personally battle with a "consumer" view of Christianity? If you haven't already done so, close this session by spending some extended time in prayer. Ask for God to help you in living for His purposes and for His glory.

---------------------------------------------------------------

---------------------------------------------------------------

---------------------------------------------------------------

## Accelerate (20 minutes that turns concepts into convictions)

**Inspiration** comes from hearing God's Word; **Motivation** grows by discussing God's Word; **Transformation** occurs when you study it for yourself.

If you want to "accelerate" your growth, here is an assignment you can do this week. To help you get the most out of this exercise, consider partnering up with somebody in your group who will also commit to do the assignment this week. Then, after you have each done the assignment, agree to spend 10 minutes by phone to share what you learned and what you are applying.

**Come Before God**

1. Read the following passage carefully and slowly.

   *Who has measured the waters in the hollow of his hand,*
   *or with the breadth of his hand marked off the heavens?*

   *Who has held the dust of the earth in a basket,*
   *or weighed the mountains on the scales*
   *and the hills in a balance?*

   *Who has understood the mind of the LORD,*
   *or instructed him as his counselor?*

   *Whom did the LORD consult to enlighten him,*
   *and who taught him the right way?*

*Who was it that taught him knowledge*
*or showed him the path of understanding?*

*Surely the nations are like a drop in a bucket;*
*they are regarded as dust on the scales;*
*he weighs the islands as though they were fine dust.*

*Do you not know?*

*Have you not heard?*

*Has it not been told you from the beginning?*

*Have you not understood since the earth was founded?*

*He sits enthroned above the circle of the earth,*
*and its people are like grasshoppers.*

*He stretches out the heavens like a canopy,*
*and spreads them out like a tent to live in.*

*He brings princes to naught*
*and reduces the rulers of this world to nothing.*

*No sooner are they planted,*
*no sooner are they sown,*
*no sooner do they take root in the ground,*

*than he blows on them and they wither,*
*and a whirlwind sweeps them away like chaff.*

*"To whom will you compare me?*
*Or who is my equal?" says the Holy One.*

*Lift your eyes and look to the heavens:*
*Who created all these?*

*He who brings out the starry host one by one,*
*and calls them each by name.*

*Because of his great power and mighty strength,*
*not one of them is missing.*

---

**ISAIAH 40:12-15, 21-26 (NIV)**

2.  From these verses in Isaiah 40, come up with as many "God is..."
    statements as possible. (i.e.  God is powerful, God is all-knowing)

    ------------------      ------------------      ------------------

    ------------------      ------------------      ------------------

    ------------------      ------------------      ------------------

3.  What attribute or characteristic of God leaves you in awe? Spend a few
    moments worshipping and thanking God for that quality.

4.  Now read Isaiah 6:1-8. What was Isaiah's response when he got a high and
    holy view of God?

    ----------------------------------------------------------------

    ----------------------------------------------------------------

    ----------------------------------------------------------------

## Do Life In Community

5.  Schedule some time this week with someone in your small group. Have an
    honest discussion about the issue of consumerism and its impact on you
    and your family. Be sure to discuss the following question – What does it
    look like to be separate from the world's values (Romans 12:2)?

## Be On Mission

6.  Decide that you will live this week with a "high view of God." Reflect on
    Isaiah 40 throughout the week and allow your view of God to impact how
    you face the challenges of the week.

# Session 3

# Where Do We Get the Power to Change?

## Part 1

# TRANS*formed*
The Miracle of Life Change

## Take It In (Watch the Video)

### Introduction – What's Wrong With Me?

> *For I desire to do what is good, but I cannot carry it out. For what I do is not the good I want to do; no the evil I do not want to do – this I keep on doing.*　　– The Apostle Paul

**ROMANS 7:19 (NIV)**

### Review – Ephesians 4:1-6

The Call to Transformation – "Walk worthy of your new life"

The Process – "Practice sacrificial, other-centered relationships"

| | | |
|---|---|---|
| Be Humble | ➡ | <u>Not</u> Proud/Selfish |
| Be Gentle | ➡ | <u>Not</u> Demanding/Harsh |
| Be Patient | ➡ | <u>Not</u> Impatient/Angry |
| Bear with | ➡ | <u>Not</u> Critical/Judgmental |
| Making every effort | ➡ | <u>Not</u> Slothful/Disengaged |

### Question –

How did Jesus conquer sin?

How does that work in my life?

### How Do We Deal With The Problem Of Sin?

**Our Text** – Ephesians 4:7-10 (NASB)

*But to each one of us grace was given according to the measure of Christ's gift. Therefore it says,*

*"WHEN HE ASCENDED ON HIGH,*
*HE LED CAPTIVE A HOST OF CAPTIVES,*
*AND HE GAVE GIFTS TO MEN."*

Now this expression, "He ascended," what does it mean except that He also had descended into the lower parts of the earth? He who descended is Himself also He who ascended far above all the heavens, so that He might fill all things.

**Key Words**

- "He led captive a host of captives" ➡ Quote from Psalm 68:18

- "the lower parts of the earth" ➡ Jewish view of the after-life;
  Luke 16

  - Hades – The Wicked – 1 Peter 3:18-19

  - Paradise – The Righteous – 1 Peter 4:6

- "that He might fill all things" ➡ Revelation 5:9-13

*Looking forward* ➡     ⬅ *Looking backward*

OT                                    NT

## Talk It Over

1. Have someone read out loud Romans 8:31-39. Spend a few minutes together in prayer and praise. Center your prayers on the good work of Jesus and the victory that is ours.

2. What stands out most to you from Chip's teaching this week?

---

---

---

3. The central figure of scripture is Jesus. Have someone in the group read Colossians 1:15-20. As a group, make a list of all the phrases that show the supremacy of Christ.

---

---

---

4. From that same passage in Colossians 1, which description of Christ's supremacy most connects to you personally? Why?

---

---

---

## Live It Out – B.I.O.

The word "bio" means "life." Found in those three simple letters — B.I.O. — is the key to helping you become the person God wants you to be.

### B = COME "BEFORE GOD" DAILY

Meet with Him personally through prayer and His word to enjoy His presence, receive His direction, and follow His will.

### I = DO LIFE "IN COMMUNITY" WEEKLY

Structure your week to personally connect in safe relationships that provide love, support, transparency, challenge, and accountability.

### O = BE "ON MISSION" 24/7

Cultivate a mindset to live out Jesus' love for others through acts of sacrifice as well as service at home, work, play, and church.

**Come Before God**

5.   Read 1 Corinthians 1:18-21; 26-31. What does this passage teach about the centrality of the cross? What most speaks to you from these verses?

_____

_____

_____

**Do Life In Community**

6.  How could this group help you to live with greater awareness of Christ's victory and your identity in Christ?

    ------------------------------------------------------------

    ------------------------------------------------------------

    ------------------------------------------------------------

**Be On Mission**

7.  2 Corinthians 5:17-21 is a great passage about what Christ has done for us and the implications for our lives. What does it mean to be Christ's ambassador? Based on your life circumstances, what can you do to represent (be an ambassador for) Christ? Get specific.

    ------------------------------------------------------------

    ------------------------------------------------------------

    ------------------------------------------------------------

## Accelerate (20 minutes that turns concepts into convictions)

**Inspiration** comes from hearing God's Word. **Motivation** grows by discussing God's Word. **Transformation** occurs when you study it for yourself.

If you want to "accelerate" your growth, here is an assignment you can do at home each week. Our convictions become even stronger when we dig into Scripture and discover truth for ourselves. To help you get the most out of this exercise, consider partnering up with someone in your group who will also commit to doing the assignment this week. Then, after you have each completed the assignment, agree to spend 10 minutes by phone sharing what you learned and what you are applying.

**Come Before God**

1. Read the following passage carefully and slowly.

   *When you were dead in your sins and in the uncircumcision of your sinful nature, God made you alive with Christ. He forgave us all our sins, having canceled the written code, with its regulations, that was against us and that stood opposed to us; he took it away, nailing it to the cross. And having disarmed the powers and authorities, he made a public spectacle of them, triumphing over them by the cross.*

   ### Colossians 2:13-15 (NIV)

2. Go through this passage and circle all the verbs that demonstrate what Christ accomplished on the cross.

3. Read Ephesians 2:1-3 for a more detailed description of what it means to be "dead in your sin".

4.  Colossians 2:15 says that Christ "disarmed the powers and authorities". From what you learned in the session from Chip this week, what does it means that Christ "disarmed the powers and authorities"?

------------------------------------------------------------

------------------------------------------------------------

------------------------------------------------------------

## Do Life In Community

5.  Get a prayer partner for this week. Commit to pray for one another that you will be able to rest in the victorious work of Christ. Also commit to meditate on passages this week that speak of the glorious work of Jesus on the cross.

## Be On Mission

6.  Commit this week to share the good news of the cross with someone. Look for an opportunity to share your faith and what Jesus has done to change your life.

Session 4

# Where Do We Get the Power to Change?

Part 2

## TRANS*formed*

The Miracle of Life Change

Take It In (Watch the video)

**The Implications for "Transforming"**

- Fact #1 - Christ is a conquering victor over sin, death, and Satan. The power to live a new life was made possible by His _____ and _____. Colossians 2:13-15, Ephesians 2:1-8

  - Principle #1 – Life Change Always Begins With The _____.

- Fact #2 – We become "co-partakers" of Christ's victory over sin, death and Satan the moment we _____ as our personal Savior by faith. Romans 6:3-11, 17-19, 22-24

  - Principle #2 – Life Change Demands We _____ On The Truth.

## US                                    GOD

| WAGES |      |       | FREE GIFT |
|-------|------|-------|-----------|
| SIN   |      |       | ETERNAL LIFE |
|       | DEATH |      |           |

*For the wages of sin are death, but the free gift of God is eternal life in Christ Jesus our Lord.*

**ROMANS 6:23**

- **Fact #3** – Every believer is given a _____ (supernatural enabling) at the moment of salvation for two reasons:

    1. To remind us that "life-change" occurs on the basis of _____ not _____.

    2. To empower us as other-centered "agents of grace" who supply what _____ to be transformed into the likeness of Christ.

    - **Principle #3** – Life Change Is Both A Gift And A _____.

## Talk It Over

1. Based on what you know about yourself, what do you believe is your spiritual gift? Have the others in the group speak into your life about this and affirm what they see in you.

    _____

    _____

    _____

2. Chip said "Life change always begins with the truth". You are free, forgiven and secure. Which of those three truths is most important for you right now? Why?

    ------------------------------------------------------------

    ------------------------------------------------------------

    ------------------------------------------------------------

3. Read Romans 6:17-18 again. Sometimes theologians speak of the fact that we have been delivered from the power and penalty of sin, but not the presence of sin. What do they mean by that statement?

    ------------------------------------------------------------

    ------------------------------------------------------------

    ------------------------------------------------------------

4. What do you think it means to be a "slave to righteousness"? If you were more conscious of being a "slave to righteousness", how would it change you?

    ------------------------------------------------------------

    ------------------------------------------------------------

    ------------------------------------------------------------

## Live It Out – B.I.O.

The word "bio" means "life." Found in those three simple letters — B.I.O. — is the key to helping you become the person God wants you to be.

### B = COME "BEFORE GOD" DAILY

Meet with Him personally through prayer and His word to enjoy His presence, receive His direction, and follow His will.

### I = DO LIFE "IN COMMUNITY" WEEKLY

Structure your week to personally connect in safe relationships that provide love, support, transparency, challenge, and accountability.

### O = BE "ON MISSION" 24/7

Cultivate a mindset to live out Jesus' love for others through acts of sacrifice as well as service at home, work, play, and church.

**Come Before God**

5. In Romans 6, Paul talks about counting ourselves dead to sin and alive to God. What do you think Paul means by that statement?

_____

_____

_____

**Do Life In Community**

6. Chip said that once we become Christians, we are "in Christ" and our identity is in Him. How much do you struggle finding your identity in Christ instead of success, people pleasing, and wealth? Share honestly with your group your journey with this issue.

**Be On Mission**

7. How can you serve others with your gift? What step do you need to take in order to put your gift into action?

---

---

---

## Accelerate (20 minutes that turn concepts into convictions)

**Inspiration** comes from hearing God's Word. **Motivation** grows by discussing God's Word. **Transformation** occurs when you study it for yourself.

If you want to "accelerate" your growth, here is an assignment you can do at home each week. Our convictions become even stronger when we dig into Scripture and discover truth for ourselves. To help you get the most out of this exercise, consider partnering up with someone in your group who will also commit to doing the assignment this week. Then, after you have each completed the assignment, agree to spend 10 minutes by phone sharing what you learned and what you are applying.

**Come Before God**

1. Read the following passage carefully and slowly.

   *What then? Shall we sin because we are not under law but under grace? By no means! Don't you know that when you offer yourselves to someone to obey him as slaves, you are slaves to the one whom you obey — whether you are slaves to sin, which leads to death, or to obedience, which leads to righteousness? But thanks be to God that, though you used to be slaves to sin, you wholeheartedly obeyed the form of teaching to which you were entrusted. You have been set free from sin and have become slaves to righteousness.*

*I put this in human terms because you are weak in your natural selves. Just as you used to offer the parts of your body in slavery to impurity and to ever-increasing wickedness, so now offer them in slavery to righteousness leading to holiness.When you were slaves to sin, you were free from the control of righteousness. What benefit did you reap at that time from the things you are now ashamed of? Those things result in death! But now that you have been set free from sin and have become slaves to God, the benefit you reap leads to holiness, and the result is eternal life. For the wages of sin is death, but the gift of God is eternal life in Christ Jesus our Lord.*

ROMANS 6:15-23 (NIV)

2.   Using the chart below, make two lists from this passage in Romans 6.

   1.   Make a list of all the words that describe the results or characteristics of being a slave to sin.

   2.   Make a list of all the words that describe the results or characteristics of being a slave to righteousness.

| Slave of sin | Slave of righteousness |
|---|---|
| 1. | 1. |
| 2. | 2. |
| 3. | 3. |
| 4. | 4. |
| 5. | 5. |
| 6. | 6. |
| 7. | 7. |
| 8. | 8. |

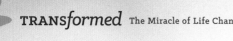

3.  Go through this passage and circle all the words that are past tense (they have already happened to you).

## Do Life In Community

4.  A mind and heart saturated with the Word of God is a prerequisite for life change. Get together with a good friend this week and share what God has been teaching you from His Word. Also, ask them for their help in keeping you accountable to consistent time in God's Word.

## Be On Mission

5.  One of the results of your salvation is that God has given you spiritual gift(s) in order to serve others. Determine to use your gift this week to serve someone.

# How to Become the Person You've Always Longed to Be

## Part 1

**TRANS*formed***

The Miracle of Life Change

Take It In (Watch the video)

**Introduction: Can You Imagine?**

- ...driving home after an exhausting and stressful day to hear an "S.O.S." voicemail from a not-so-close friend...and immediately experiencing a shift of focus off yourself and your stressful day and finding yourself filled with compassion and energy to help this person in need?

- ...hearing of a promotion or a financial windfall in the life of your ex-husband/wife...and having the first thoughts that come to your mind be joy and gratitude to God for His blessing on their life?

- ...being able to hear the honest conversations of your children and your closest friends as they've gathered at your home after your funeral... describing you as the most patient, loyal, and Christ-like person they had ever known?

**How God Brings Out The Best In His Children:**

*And He gave some as apostles, and some as prophets, and some as evangelists, and some as pastors and teachers, for the equipping of the saints for the work of service, to the building up of the body of Christ; until we all attain to the unity of the faith, and of the knowledge of the Son of God, to a mature man, to the measure of the stature which belongs to the fullness of Christ. As a result we are no longer to be children, tossed here and there by waves and carried about by every wind of doctrine, by the trickery of men, by craftiness in deceitful scheming; but speaking the truth in love, we are to grow up in all aspects into Him, who is the head, even Christ, from whom the whole body, being fitted and held together by what every joint supplies, according to the proper working of each individual part, causes the growth of the body for the building up of itself in love.*

EPHESIANS 4:11-16 (NASB)

1. Leaders are gifted to _____ God's people for service. (Ephesians 4:11-12a)

2. Every member is a _____. (Ephesians 4:12)

## Talk It Over

1. Share about a time when you were most fulfilled in serving and using your gifts. How has your involvement in ministry impacted your personal spiritual growth?

   _____

   _____

   _____

2. Chip said "transformation in the church requires an equipping mindset both by leaders and by people." How would you assess the "equipping mindset" in your church?

   _____

   _____

   _____

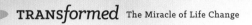

3. Who has played a significant role in your life by investing in you and equipping you? What did they do that impacted you?

_____

_____

_____

4. 1 Peter 4:10 (NASB) says, "As each one has received a special gift, employ it in serving one another as good stewards of the manifold grace of God." For you personally, what do you need to do in order to be a good "steward" of the spiritual gifts God has given you?

_____

_____

_____

## Live It Out — B.I.O.

The word "bio" means "life." Found in those three simple letters — B.I.O. — is the key to helping you become the person God wants you to be.

### B = COME "BEFORE GOD" DAILY
Meet with Him personally through prayer and His word to enjoy His presence, receive His direction, and follow His will.

### I = DO LIFE "IN COMMUNITY" WEEKLY
Structure your week to personally connect in safe relationships that provide love, support, transparency, challenge, and accountability.

## O = BE "ON MISSION" 24/7

Cultivate a mindset to live out Jesus' love for others through acts of sacrifice as well as service at home, work, play, and church.

### Come Before God

5.  Read Romans 12:3-8. From this passage, what are some valuable principles we can learn when it comes to exercising our gifts?

    _____

    _____

    _____

### Do Life In Community

6.  How can you use your gifts and abilities to minister within your own small group?

    _____

    _____

    _____

**Be On Mission**

7. Who is it that you should be investing in and equipping? What next step will you take to engage them?

_____

_____

_____

## Accelerate (20 minutes that turn concepts into convictions)

**Inspiration** comes from hearing God's Word. **Motivation** grows by discussing God's Word. **Transformation** occurs when you study it for yourself.

If you want to "accelerate" your growth, here is an assignment you can do at home each week. Our convictions become even stronger when we dig into Scripture and discover truth for ourselves. To help you get the most out of this exercise, consider partnering up with someone in your group who will also commit to doing the assignment this week. Then, after you have each completed the assignment, agree to spend 10 minutes by phone sharing what you learned and what you are applying.

**Come Before God**

1. Read the following passage carefully and slowly.

   _The body is a unit, though it is made up of many parts; and though all its parts are many, they form one body. So it is with Christ. For we were all baptized by one Spirit into one body—whether Jews or Greeks, slave or free —and we were all given the one Spirit to drink. Now the body is not made up of one part but of many. If the foot should say, "Because I am not a hand, I do not belong to the body," it would not for that reason cease to be part of the body. And if the ear should say, "Because I am not an eye, I do_ *not belong to the body," it would not for that reason cease to be part of the body. If the whole body were an eye, where would the sense of hearing be? If the whole body were an ear, where would the sense of smell be? But in fact God has arranged the parts in the body, every one of them, just as he wanted them to be. If they were all one part, where would the body be? As it is, there are many parts, but one body. The eye cannot say to the hand, "I don't need you!" And the head cannot say to the feet, "I don't need you!" On the contrary, those parts of the body that seem to be weaker are indispensable, and the parts that we think are less honorable we treat with special honor. And the parts that are unpresentable are treated with special modesty, while our presentable parts need no special treatment. But God has combined the members of the body and has given greater honor to the parts that lacked it, so that there should be no division in the body, but that its parts should have equal concern for each other. If one part suffers, every part suffers with it; if one part is honored, every part rejoices with it.*

1 CORINTHIANS 12:12-26 (NIV)

2.  According to verse 18, who is responsible for distributing spiritual gifts? How does that truth impact your attitude toward your gifting?

    ----------------------------------------------------------------

    ----------------------------------------------------------------

    ----------------------------------------------------------------

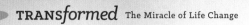

3.  Why is the "physical body" a good word picture of the church and the way it should function?

    _____

    _____

    _____

4.  From this passage, what are some principles you can draw out that help in the understanding and exercise of gifts within the body of Christ, i.e. There is no room for feelings of superiority in the church (v.21)?

    _____

    _____

    _____

## Do Life In Community

5.  In order to develop and grow in your gifts, who is it that you could learn from? Set up a lunch with them and learn all you can from their experience and expertise.

## Be On Mission

6.  During the group session this week, you were asked who you should be investing in and equipping. Commit to contact them this week and taking the next step to invest in them.

Session 6

# How to Become the Person You've Always Longed to Be

Part 2

## TRANS*formed*

The Miracle of Life Change

## Take It In (Watch the video)

**Review from week 5**

1. Leaders are gifted to equip God's people for service. (Ephesians 4:11-12a)

2. Every member is a minister. (Ephesians 4:12)

3. _____ are developed to help _____ _____ to live everyday in every way just as Jesus would live if He were living out His life in their physical body. (Ephesians 4:13)

4. God measures spiritual maturity by specific, _____ criteria (Ephesians 4:14-16):

   • Doctrinal Stability

   • Authentic Relationships

   • Full Participation

   • Growing Love

**Are You Positioning Yourself For God To Bring Out The Best In You?**

A Diagnostic Evaluation:

1. I am currently being equipped for ministry by:

   O   Worshipping regularly

   O   Listening/reading for personal growth

   O   Being involved in an apprenticeship and/or mentoring relationship

2.  I am currently ministering and building into the lives of others:

    O   Rarely or sporadically

    O   Functioning in my gifts with joy and fruitfulness

    O   Involved in ministry, but don't feel deeply useful

    O   Regularly seeing other's lives changed through me and my gifts

3.  I am becoming more like Christ in my everyday life as evidenced by:

    O   Coming <u>Before God</u> daily

    O   A desire to read God's Word

    O   A disciplined study and understanding of God's Word

    O   An ability to "see through" false teaching

4.  I am becoming more like Christ in my everyday life as evidenced by:

    O   Doing life <u>In Community</u>

    O   Enjoying one or more deep, authentic relationships in Christ

    O   My regular attendance in small group where "speaking the truth in love" is common

    O   Having three or four gut-level accountability relationships that are helping me through the most sensitive areas of my life

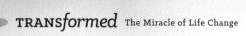

5. I am becoming more like Christ in my everyday life as evidenced by:

    O   Being <u>On Mission</u> 24/7

    O   A desire to become more deeply involved in serving God's people (worship, classes, friendships, meeting needs)

    O   A sense of belonging and acceptance with my church family

    O   A clear sense that I "fit" in my church body (I am loved by others and find myself caring and helping them in increasing measure)

## Talk It Over

1. Take the Diagnostic Evaluation that is in your study guide. Share with the group a statement you checked that you couldn't have a year or two ago. Also, share with the group how you think you have grown (improved) in that area.

2. Look through your diagnostic test and identify the one area where you most need to grow. Now, share that area where you want and need God to change you.

3. If time and money were no limitation, what kind of ministry would you dream of being involved in?

------------------------------------------------------------

------------------------------------------------------------

------------------------------------------------------------

4. Chip said that one of the evidences of maturity is "full participation" in the body of Christ. How would you describe your participation in the body of Christ? Is there any barrier keeping you from participating more fully

_____

_____

_____

## Live It Out – B.I.O.

The word "bio" means "life." Found in those three simple letters — B.I.O. — is the key to helping you become the person God wants you to be.

**B = COME "BEFORE GOD" DAILY**
Meet with Him personally through prayer and His word to enjoy His presence, receive His direction, and follow His will.

**I = DO LIFE "IN COMMUNITY" WEEKLY**
Structure your week to personally connect in safe relationships that provide love, support, transparency, challenge, and accountability.

**O = BE "ON MISSION" 24/7**
Cultivate a mindset to live out Jesus' love for others through acts of sacrifice as well as service at home, work, play, and church.

**Come Before God**

5.  Read John 13:35; Ephesians 5:2; Colossian 3:14. Do an honest assessment at how you've been doing at growing in love. Where do you have the most trouble being loving?

    ------------------------------------------------------------

    ------------------------------------------------------------

    ------------------------------------------------------------

**Do Life In Community**

6.  One of the evidences of maturity is authentic relationships. Read Romans 12:9-16 and discuss which of the characteristics listed is the one your group does best. And, then, discuss which characteristic your group needs to work on.

**Be On Mission**

7.  Who could you show love to this week that is far from God? What step will you take to make it happen?

    ------------------------------------------------------------

    ------------------------------------------------------------

    ------------------------------------------------------------

Accelerate (20 minutes that turn concepts into convictions)

**Inspiration** comes from hearing God's Word. **Motivation** grows by discussing God's Word. **Transformation** occurs when you study it for yourself.

If you want to "accelerate" your growth, here is an assignment you can do at home each week. Our convictions become even stronger when we dig into Scripture and discover truth for ourselves. To help you get the most out of this exercise, consider partnering up with someone in your group who will also commit to doing the assignment this week. Then, after you have each completed the assignment, agree to spend 10 minutes by phone sharing what you learned and what you are applying.

**Come Before God**

1.   Read the following passage carefully and slowly.

> It was he who gave some to be apostles, some to be prophets, some
> to be evangelists, and some to be pastors and teachers, to prepare
> God's people for works of service, so that the body of Christ may be
> built up until we all reach unity in the faith and in the knowledge
> of the Son of God and become mature, attaining to the whole
> measure of the fullness of Christ. Then we will no longer be infants,
> tossed back and forth by the waves, and blown here and there by
> every wind of teaching and by the cunning and craftiness of men
> in their deceitful scheming. Instead, speaking the truth in love, we
> will in all things grow up into him who is the Head, that is, Christ.
> From him the whole body, joined and held together by every
> supporting ligament, grows and builds itself up in love, as each
> part does its work.

**EPHESIANS 4:11-16**

2.   Much of this passage has to do with spiritual maturity. Go back through this passage and circle all of the elements that lead toward spiritual maturity.

3. In verse 13, Paul speaks of the goal of "unity in the faith". Read John 17:20–24 and circle all of the phrases that help define true biblical unity.

4. Read Colossians 2:6-7 to discover some other marks of a maturing follower of Jesus.

## Do Life In Community

5. Schedule a time with someone in your group this week, and do a review of the Diagnostic Checkup you took in your group meeting this week. Commit to help and pray for each other.

## Be On Mission

6. In light of your Diagnostic Checkup, what step of obedience do you need to take?

--------------------------------------------------------------------

--------------------------------------------------------------------

--------------------------------------------------------------------

Session 7

# How to "Break Out" of a Destructive Cycle

Part 1

**TRANS*formed***

The Miracle of Life Change

**Introduction: "A Tale of Two Butterflies"**

A New Life Always _____ a New Lifestyle

2 Corinthians 5:17

**WARNING: Two Common Errors to Avoid**

1.  Moralism

2.  Antinomianism

**A Believer Whose Life Does Not Change = An Oxymoron**

*So I tell you this, and insist on it in the Lord, that you must no longer live as the Gentiles do, in the futility of their thinking. They are darkened in their understanding and separated from the life of God because of the ignorance that is in them due to the hardening of their hearts. Having lost all sensitivity, they have given themselves over to sensuality so as to indulge in every kind of impurity, with a continual lust for more. You, however, did not come to know Christ that way. Surely you heard of him and were taught in him in accordance with the truth that is in Jesus. You were taught, with regard to your former way of life, to put off your old self, which is being corrupted by its deceitful desires; to be made new in the attitude of your minds; and to put on the new self, created to be like God in true righteousness and holiness.*

### EPHESIANS 4:17-24 (NIV)

1.  As believers, our lives must be progressively characterized by _____ _____. (Ephesians 4:17-19)

## Talk It Over

1.  When you hear the phrase "Christian lifestyle", what does that mean for you personally? Be as specific as possible. What does it look like practically for you to have a Christian lifestyle?

    _____

    _____

    _____

2. Why do you think the Apostle Paul presented such a vivid and dark picture of life outside of Christ (Ephesians 4:17-19) even though he was writing to believers?

---

---

---

3. Have someone in the group read out loud 1 Peter 1:13-16. How would you define "holiness"? And, what does it mean to live a "holy life"?

---

---

---

**If you have men and women in your group, separate the group now by women and men for the rest of the discussion time.**

4. One error that Chip talked about avoiding is the error of moralism (legalism). When you think about your spiritual background, how much was legalism a part of your past? What was the impact?

---

---

---

## Live It Out — B.I.O.

The word "bio" means "life." Found in those three simple letters — B.I.O. — is the key to helping you become the person God wants you to be.

### B = COME "BEFORE GOD" DAILY

Meet with Him personally through prayer and His word to enjoy His presence, receive His direction, and follow His will.

### I = DO LIFE "IN COMMUNITY" WEEKLY

Structure your week to personally connect in safe relationships that provide love, support, transparency, challenge, and accountability.

### O = BE "ON MISSION" 24/7

Cultivate a mindset to live out Jesus' love for others through acts of sacrifice as well as service at home, work, play, and church.

**Come Before God**

5.  From the teaching in this session, is there some area where you are not living in obedience or purity?

_____

_____

_____

**Do Life In Community**

6.   How can the people in this group help you as you strive to live a life of moral purity?

-------------------------------------------------------------

-------------------------------------------------------------

-------------------------------------------------------------

**Be On Mission**

7.   Is there any step you need to take in order to make sure your testimony in the world is morally pure? Don't just think of blatant sin, but also more subtle, culturally acceptable compromises.

-------------------------------------------------------------

-------------------------------------------------------------

-------------------------------------------------------------

Accelerate (20 minutes that turn concepts into convictions)

**Inspiration** comes from hearing God's Word. **Motivation** grows by discussing God's Word. **Transformation** occurs when you study it for yourself.

If you want to "accelerate" your growth, here is an assignment you can do at home each week. Our convictions become even stronger when we dig into Scripture and discover truth for ourselves. To help you get the most out of this exercise, consider partnering up with someone in your group who will also commit to doing the assignment this week. Then, after you have each completed the assignment, agree to spend 10 minutes by phone sharing what you learned and what you are applying.

**Come Before God**

1.  Read the following passage carefully and slowly.

    *Since, then, you have been raised with Christ, set your hearts on things above, where Christ is seated at the right hand of God. Set your minds on things above, not on earthly things. For you died, and your life is now hidden with Christ in God. When Christ, who is your life, appears, then you also will appear with him in glory.*

    *Put to death, therefore, whatever belongs to your earthly nature: sexual immorality, impurity, lust, evil desires and greed, which is idolatry. Because of these, the wrath of God is coming. You used to walk in these ways, in the life you once lived. But now you must rid yourselves of all such things as these: anger, rage, malice, slander, and filthy language from your lips. Do not lie to each other, since you have taken off your old self with its practices and have put on the new self, which is being renewed in knowledge in the image of its Creator. Here there is no Greek or Jew, circumcised or uncircumcised, barbarian, Scythian, slave or free, but Christ is all, and is in all.*

    COLOSSIANS 3:1-10 (NIV)

2.  In verses 5-9, what are the words or phrases that are synonymous with the phrase "put to death"?

    ------------------------------------------------------------

    ------------------------------------------------------------

    ------------------------------------------------------------

3.  From this passage, make a list of the positive things that we can do or have been done for us that help us live the life God wants us to live.

4.  Go through the passage and circle all of the sins that have to do with our words (language). Then, go through the passage and underline all of the sins that have to do with our mind and thoughts.

## Do Life In Community

5.  Get together with someone from your group this week and read together this passage from Colossians 3:1-10. Then, talk about which of the sins listed in verses 5-9 are the biggest temptation for you. Commit to pray for each other this week regarding this temptation.

## Be On Mission

6.  Notice in Colossians 3:5 that Paul tells us to "put to death" whatever belongs to our old earthly nature. He doesn't tell us to manage, hide, or gloss over it. So, what step do you need to take to ruthlessly eliminate that which could be damaging to your relationship with God and your testimony in the world?

---------------------------------------------------------------

---------------------------------------------------------------

---------------------------------------------------------------

Session 8

# How to "Break Out" of a Destructive Cycle

Part 2

**TRANS*formed***

The Miracle of Life Change

## Take It In (Watch the video)

**Review from session 7**

1. As believers, our lives must be progressively characterized by moral purity. (Ephesians 4:17-19)

2. An _____ is inconceivable for us believers for two reasons:

    a) It contradicts _____ we are! (Ephesians 4:20)

    b) It contradicts _____ Christ is? (Ephesians 4:21)

3. We achieve _____ by following God's three-fold principles of transformation. (Ephesians 4:2-24)

    a) "Put-off" (point in time) **the old!**

    b) _____ (continuously) in the spirit of your mind?

    c) "Put-on" (point in time) **the new!**

## Talk It Over

1. How are you doing at renewing your mind? What steps do you need to take so that you can more consistently put Scripture into your mind?

    _____

    _____

    _____

2.  Based on this teaching from Ephesians 4, what habit, behavior, or attitude do you need to "put off"?

    ---------------------------------------------------------------

    ---------------------------------------------------------------

    ---------------------------------------------------------------

3.  Chip said "We think sin is a behavioral problem. But it really is a relational problem." What is your reaction to that statement?

    ---------------------------------------------------------------

    ---------------------------------------------------------------

    ---------------------------------------------------------------

4.  Based on this teaching from Ephesians 4, what do you need to "put on"?

    ---------------------------------------------------------------

    ---------------------------------------------------------------

    ---------------------------------------------------------------

## Live It Out — B.I.O.

The word "bio" means "life." Found in those three simple letters — B.I.O. — is the key to helping you become the person God wants you to be.

**B = COME "BEFORE GOD" DAILY**
Meet with Him personally through prayer and His word to enjoy His presence, receive His direction, and follow His will.

**I = DO LIFE "IN COMMUNITY" WEEKLY**
Structure your week to personally connect in safe relationships that provide love, support, transparency, challenge, and accountability.

**O = BE "ON MISSION" 24/7**
Cultivate a mindset to live out Jesus' love for others through acts of sacrifice as well as service at home, work, play, and church.

### Come Before God

5.  Read 2 Peter 1:3-9. Which one of the qualities listed in verses 5-7 do you want to "put on"? Why did you select the one you did?

_____

_____

_____

### Do Life In Community

6.  As a group, select a verse that you will all memorize together. As you see each other throughout the week, check in on each other and see how the Scripture memory is coming. You might want to consider having the group memorize Romans 12:1-2.

**Be On Mission**

7.  Close this session with a time of praying for each other.

Accelerate (20 minutes that turn concepts into convictions)

**Inspiration** comes from hearing God's Word. **Motivation** grows by discussing God's Word. **Transformation** occurs when you study it for yourself.

If you want to "accelerate" your growth, here is an assignment you can do at home each week or use your streaming code found in the front of your study guide. Our convictions become even stronger when we dig into Scripture and discover truth for ourselves. To help you get the most out of this exercise, consider partnering up with someone in your group who will also commit to doing the assignment this week. Then, after you have each completed the assignment, agree to spend 10 minutes by phone sharing what you learned and what you are applying.

**Come Before God**

1.  Read the following passage carefully and slowly.

    *His divine power has given us everything we need for life and godliness through our knowledge of him who called us by his own glory and goodness. Through these he has given us his very great and precious promises, so that through them you may participate in the divine nature and escape the corruption in the world caused by evil desires.*

    *For this very reason, make every effort to add to your faith goodness; and to goodness, knowledge; and to knowledge, self-control; and to self-control, perseverance; and to perseverance, godliness; and to godliness, brotherly kindness; and to brotherly kindness, love. For if you possess these qualities in increasing measure, they will keep you from being ineffective and unproductive in your knowledge of our Lord Jesus Christ. But if anyone does not have them, he is nearsighted and blind, and has forgotten that he has been cleansed from his past sins.*

    2 PETER 1:3-9 (NIV)

2. According to verse 3, what has God given you to be able to live the Christian life?

------------------------------------------------

------------------------------------------------

------------------------------------------------

3. Verse 4 says that these precious promises have been given in part so that we may "participate in the divine nature". What does that mean?

------------------------------------------------

------------------------------------------------

------------------------------------------------

4. Assess your own spiritual life against the words listed in verse 5-7. Which one of these is God calling you to "add to your faith"?

------------------------------------------------

------------------------------------------------

------------------------------------------------

5. Verse 9 says that if anyone does not have these qualities, they are "nearsighted and blind". What is Peter trying to communicate with those terms?

_____

_____

_____

## Do Life In Community

6. Have an honest conversation with your spouse or a good friend about the three culturally-acceptable destructive behaviors – materialism, people-pleasing, and workaholism. Talk about the negative impact these have had on you and what changes you will make to "put off" these destructive behaviors.

## Be On Mission

7. What step of obedience and faith is God calling you to take from this passage?

_____

_____

_____

Session 9

# The Role of Spiritual Training in the Transformation Process

## Part 1

**TRANS*formed***

The Miracle of Life Change

Take It In (Watch the video)

**Introduction — "Dad, I'm trying as hard as I can."**

Review:

1. **Every believer** is called to "be transformed" (Ephesians 4:1-6)

2. **Christ's defeat** of sin, death and Satan makes "transformation" possible. (Ephesians 4:7-10)

3. **The Church** is God's primary agent of "transforming" our lives. (Ephesians 4:11-16)

4. We achieve personal purity by God's **three-fold principles of transformation**. (Ephesians 4:17-24)

    a. "Put-off"

    b. Be renewed

    c. "Put-on"

5. **Transformation** is a matter of spiritual training vs. trying harder. (Ephesians 4:25-32)

**Five Habits that Cultivate Holiness from the Heart**

1. _____ _____

    Speak the truth in love.

*... but speaking the truth in love, we are to grow up in all aspects into Him who is the head, even Christ, Therefore, laying aside falsehood, SPEAK TRUTH EACH ONE of you WITH HIS NEIGHBOR, for we are members of one another.*

EPHESIANS 4:25 (NASB)

**Spiritual Training Station #1**

O   Training Objective:

Honesty (Personal Integrity)

O   Training Command:

"Speak the _____ in love"

(see Ephesians 4:15, 25)

O   Training Actions:

Put off – falsehood

Renew – recognize your _____ membership in God's family

Put on – truthful speech and authenticity

## Talk It Over

1.  Where do you need to go into training? Share that area and some first steps you need to start the training process.

    ----------------------------------------------------------------

    ----------------------------------------------------------------

    ----------------------------------------------------------------

2.  How would you define the word "integrity"? Share a story from your life when your integrity was tested.

    ----------------------------------------------------------------

    ----------------------------------------------------------------

    ----------------------------------------------------------------

3.  Share a time when someone was honest and spoke the truth in love to you. How did it impact you?

    ----------------------------------------------------------------

    ----------------------------------------------------------------

    ----------------------------------------------------------------

4. Chip spoke about being honest or having integrity in the "little things". What "little thing" can tempt you to compromise your integrity?

_____

_____

_____

## Live It Out — B.I.O.

The word "bio" means "life." Found in those three simple letters — B.I.O. — is the key to helping you become the person God wants you to be.

### B = COME "BEFORE GOD" DAILY
Meet with Him personally through prayer and His word to enjoy His presence, receive His direction, and follow His will.

### I = DO LIFE "IN COMMUNITY" WEEKLY
Structure your week to personally connect in safe relationships that provide love, support, transparency, challenge, and accountability.

### O = BE "ON MISSION" 24/7
Cultivate a mindset to live out Jesus' love for others through acts of sacrifice as well as service at home, work, play, and church.

## Come Before God

5.  James 5:16 (NIV) says:

    *Therefore confess your sins to each other and pray for each other*
    *so that you may be healed. The prayer of a righteous man is*
    *powerful and effective.*

    What does this verse teach us about confession? What is most difficult for
    you in following this command?

    _____

    _____

    _____

## Do Life In Community

6.  In Ephesians 4:25, Paul said:

    *Therefore, laying aside falsehood, SPEAK TRUTH EACH ONE of*
    *you WITH HIS NEIGHBOR, for we are members of one another.*

    Why do you think Paul connected honesty with the statement "for we are
    members of one another"?

    _____

    _____

    _____

**Be On Mission**

7.  What are some practical ways that Christians could be more honest and therefore help their testimony to unbelievers?

_____

_____

_____


Accelerate (20 minutes that turn concepts into convictions)

**Inspiration** comes from hearing God's Word. **Motivation** grows by discussing God's Word. **Transformation** occurs when you study it for yourself.

If you want to "accelerate" your growth, here is an assignment you can do at home each week. Our convictions become even stronger when we dig into Scripture and discover truth for ourselves. To help you get the most out of this exercise, consider partnering up with someone in your group who will also commit to doing the assignment this week. Then, after you have each completed the assignment, agree to spend 10 minutes by phone sharing what you learned and what you are applying.


**Come Before God**

1.  Read the following passage carefully and slowly.

    _Who may worship in your sanctuary, LORD? Who may enter your presence on your holy hill? Those who lead blameless lives and do what is right, speaking the truth from sincere hearts. Those who refuse to gossip or harm their neighbors or speak evil of their friends. Those who despise flagrant sinners, and honor the faithful followers of the LORD, and keep their promises even when it hurts. Those who lend money without charging interest, and who cannot be bribed to lie about the innocent. Such people will stand firm forever._

    **PSALM 15 (NLT)**

2. What do you think the Psalmist is trying to communicate by using the word pictures of the "sanctuary" and "holy hill"?

---------------------------------------------------------------

---------------------------------------------------------------

---------------------------------------------------------------

3. Sometimes integrity is about what we "do" and sometimes integrity is about what we "don't do". Go through this passage and circle the words that are about things we "do". Then, go back through the passage and underline the words that indicate the things we "don't" do if we have integrity.

4. Proverbs 11:3 (NIV) says:

*The integrity of the upright guides them, but the unfaithful are destroyed by their duplicity.*

How is integrity a kind of roadmap for life? Work to memorize this verse this week.

---------------------------------------------------------------

---------------------------------------------------------------

---------------------------------------------------------------

## Do Life In Community

5.  This week schedule lunch with a trusted friend. Consider reading this passage together over lunch and then having a discussion about the "little things" where you can get tripped up in your integrity. Then, pray for one another and commit to help each other in your pursuit of integrity.

## Be On Mission

6.  In the teaching this past week, Chip talked about the power of confession. Determine that this week when you blow it, you will "own your stuff" and confess and make it right.

Session 10

# The Role of Spiritual Training in the Transformation Process

Part 2

**TRANS*formed***

The Miracle of Life Change

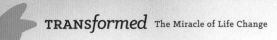

Take It In (Watch the video)

Review from Session 9

**Spiritual Training Station #1**

    O   **Training Objective:**

          Honesty (Personal Integrity)

    O   **Training Command:**

          "Speak the truth in love"

          (see Ephesians 4:15, 25)

    O   **Training Actions:**

          Put off – falsehood

          Renew – recognize your shared membership in God's family

          Put on – truthful speech and authenticity

O   **Training Apparatus:**

Practice _____.


2.   _____


**Deal with anger appropriately.**


> *BE ANGRY, AND yet DO NOT SIN; do not let the sun go down on your anger, and do not give the devil an opportunity.*
>
> ───────────────────────────────
>
> EPHESIANS 4:26-27 (NASB)


**Spiritual Training Session #2**


O   **Training Objective:**

Emotional Control


O   **Training Command:**

"Be angry and yet do not sin"

(see Ephesians 4:26)

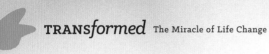 

O      **Training Actions:**

Put off – anger that leads to sin and offense

Renew – recognize the dangers of _____ anger

Put on – appropriate expressions of anger

O      **Training Apparatus:**

Practice "I _____" Messages

Make _____ requests

## Talk It Over

1.   For you personally, what was the biggest takeaway from today's teaching on anger?

_____

_____

_____

2.   When you look around at our world, what do you have "righteous anger" about?

_____

_____

_____

3.  In your opinion, when does "righteous anger" become "unrighteous anger"?

    -------------------------------------------------------------

    -------------------------------------------------------------

    -------------------------------------------------------------

4.  In what situations do you most struggle with the issue of anger?

    -------------------------------------------------------------

    -------------------------------------------------------------

    -------------------------------------------------------------

## Live It Out — B.I.O.

The word "bio" means "life." Found in those three simple letters — B.I.O. — is the key to helping you become the person God wants you to be.

### B = COME "BEFORE GOD" DAILY
Meet with Him personally through prayer and His word to enjoy His presence, receive His direction, and follow His will.

### I = DO LIFE "IN COMMUNITY" WEEKLY
Structure your week to personally connect in safe relationships that provide love, support, transparency, challenge, and accountability.

### O = BE "ON MISSION" 24/7
Cultivate a mindset to live out Jesus' love for others through acts of sacrifice as well as service at home, work, play, and church.

## Come Before God

5.     James 1:19-20 says:

> *My dear brothers and sisters, take note of this: Everyone should be quick to listen, slow to speak and slow to become angry, because human anger does not produce the righteousness that God desires.*

James challenges us to be quick to listen, slow to speak and slow to become angry. Which of those three do you most need to work on? What practical step could you take?

_____

_____

_____

## Do Life In Community

6.     Part of living in authentic community is learning to deal with anger. How do you typically express anger? Are you more of a spewer or a stuffer? And, how are you doing at not letting the "sun go down on your anger"?

_____

_____

_____

**Be On Mission**

7.   How well do you use "I feel" messages and how well are you doing at making direct requests?

_____

_____

_____

## Accelerate (20 minutes that turn concepts into convictions)

**Inspiration** comes from hearing God's Word. **Motivation** grows by discussing God's Word. **Transformation** occurs when you study it for yourself.

If you want to "accelerate" your growth, here is an assignment you can do at home each week. Our convictions become even stronger when we dig into Scripture and discover truth for ourselves. To help you get the most out of this exercise, consider partnering up with someone in your group who will also commit to doing the assignment this week. Then, after you have each completed the assignment, agree to spend 10 minutes by phone sharing what you learned and what you are applying.

**Come Before God**

1.   Read the following passage carefully and slowly.

*You have heard that it was said to the people long ago, 'You shall not murder, and anyone who murders will be subject to judgment.' But I tell you that anyone who is angry with a brother or sister will be subject to judgment. Again, anyone who says to a brother or sister, 'Raca,' is answerable to the court. And anyone who says, 'You fool!' will be in danger of the fire of hell.*

*Therefore, if you are offering your gift at the altar and there remember that your brother or sister has something against you, leave your gift there in front of the altar. First go and be reconciled to them; then come and offer your gift.*

*Settle matters quickly with your adversary who is taking you to court. Do it while you are still together on the way, or your adversary may hand you over to the judge, and the judge may hand you over to the officer, and you may be thrown into prison. Truly I tell you, you will not get out until you have paid the last penny.*

**MATTHEW 5:21-25 (NIV)**

2. According to verse 22, what are the different kinds of consequences listed for anger? Why do you think Jesus speaks of such harsh and dramatic judgment for anger?

----------------------------------------------------------------

----------------------------------------------------------------

----------------------------------------------------------------

3. From verses 23 and 24, make a list of the steps someone is to take if there is a relational problem.

- ----------------------------------------------------------

- ----------------------------------------------------------

- ----------------------------------------------------------

- ----------------------------------------------------------

4.   In verse 25, why do you think Jesus tells us to "settle matters quickly"? What happens when we delay and procrastinate?

_____

_____

_____

## Do Life In Community

5.   Have a conversation with your spouse or a good friend this week. Ask them where they see anger show up in your life and then ask for their help in keeping you accountable for your anger.

## Be On Mission

6.   Is there any relationship in your life where there is unresolved bitterness and anger? Spend a few moments in prayer and reflection, asking God to bring to mind anyone where there is a fractured relationship. If God does bring someone to mind, take the necessary steps to seek restoration of the relationship.

# Session 11

# The Power of Spiritual Training in the Transformation Process

## Part 1

**TRANS*formed***

The Miracle of Life Change

**Intro — Transformation is a "joint effort"**

*You are the God who performs miracles; you display your power among the peoples.*

---

PSALM 77:14 (NIV)

*The Spirit of God, who raised Jesus from the dead, lives in you... Therefore dear brothers and sisters, you have no obligation to do what your sinful nature urges you to do.*

---

ROMANS 8: 11,12 (NIV)

*I can do all things through Christ who strengthens me.*

---

PHILIPPIANS 4:13 (NIV)

*...work out your salvation with fear and trembling; for it is God who is at work in you, both to will and to work for His good pleasure.*

---

PHILIPPIANS 2:12-13 (NASB)

3. _____ _____- Work hard; refuse to take "short cuts."

*He who steals must steal no longer; but rather he must labor, performing with his own hands what is good, so that he will have something to share with one who has need.*

---

EPHESIANS 4:28 (NASB)

## Spiritual Training Station #3

○ **Training Objective**:

Financial Stewardship (Work Ethic)

○ **Training Command**:

"_____ no longer"

(see Ephesians 4:28)

○ **Training Actions**:

Put off – stealing

Renew – recognize the _____ and _____ of work

Put on – work unto _____  _____.
Colossians 3:23-24 (NIV)

○ **Training Apparatus**:

Write out your "_____ _____" list

4.   _____ _____- Don't wound with your words.

*Let no unwholesome word proceed from your mouth, but only such a word as is good for edification according to the need of the moment, so that it will give grace to those who hear. Do not grieve the Holy Spirit of God, by whom you were sealed for the day of redemption.*

EPHESIANS 4:29-30 (NASB)

**Spiritual Training Session #4**

○ **Training Objective:**

Positive Speech

○ **Train Command:**

"Say only what helps"

(the message of Ephesians 4:29)

○ **Training Actions:**

Put off – negative speech

Renew – recognize the _____ and _____ of your speech (Proverbs 18:21, Luke 6:45, Matthew 12:36-37)

Put on – positive, encouraging speech

## Talk It Over

1.  Who was a person in your life that believed in you and spoke words of faith about what you could be? Then, share with the group what that person said and did to encourage you.

    _____

    _____

    _____

2.  When you look back on your early years, what was modeled for you in terms of "work ethic"? What kind of impact has that had on you?

    _____

    _____

    _____

3.  Have someone in the group read out loud Ephesians 6:5-8. What can we learn from this passage about how we are to do our work?

    _____

    _____

    _____

4.  Chip said that the training apparatus for "diligence" is to develop a "to be" list. What are one or two statements you would want on your "to be" list?

---

---

---

## Live It Out – B.I.O.

The word "bio" means "life." Found in those three simple letters — B.I.O. — is the key to helping you become the person God wants you to be.

### B = COME "BEFORE GOD" DAILY
Meet with Him personally through prayer and His word to enjoy His presence, receive His direction, and follow His will.

### I = DO LIFE "IN COMMUNITY" WEEKLY
Structure your week to personally connect in safe relationships that provide love, support, transparency, challenge, and accountability.

### O = BE "ON MISSION" 24/7
Cultivate a mindset to live out Jesus' love for others through acts of sacrifice as well as service at home, work, play, and church.

**Come Before God**

5.  In Luke 6:45 (NIV), Jesus said:

*A good man brings good things out of the good stored up in his heart, and an evil man brings evil things out of the evil stored up in his heart. For the mouth speaks what the heart is full of.*

Chip mentioned several specific kinds of negative speech that can come out of our heart: Sarcasm, put down, innuendo, put down, negativity, outburst of anger, criticism, labeling, abusive speech, cussing, swearing, taking the Lord's name in vain, slander, gossip, and coarse jokes.

Which of these can you be most tempted to engage in?

----------------------------------------------------------------

----------------------------------------------------------------

----------------------------------------------------------------

## Do Life In Community

6. In what practical ways can your group help you control your tongue and be more positive with your words?

----------------------------------------------------------------

----------------------------------------------------------------

----------------------------------------------------------------

## Be On Mission

7. Think of someone you know that doesn't know Christ. How could you bless them with your words this coming week?

----------------------------------------------------------------

----------------------------------------------------------------

----------------------------------------------------------------

Accelerate (20 minutes that turn concepts into convictions)

**Inspiration** comes from hearing God's Word. **Motivation** grows by discussing God's Word. **Transformation** occurs when you study it for yourself.

If you want to "accelerate" your growth, here is an assignment you can do at home each week. Our convictions become even stronger when we dig into Scripture and discover truth for ourselves. To help you get the most out of this exercise, consider partnering up with someone in your group who will also commit to doing the assignment this week. Then, after you have each completed the assignment, agree to spend 10 minutes by phone sharing what you learned and what you are applying.

**Come Before God**

1.  Read the following passage carefully and slowly.

    *He who has been stealing must steal no longer, but must work, doing something useful with his own hands, that he may have something to share with those in need. Do not let any unwholesome talk come out of your mouths, but only what is helpful for building others up according to their needs, that it may benefit those who listen. And do not grieve the Holy Spirit of God, with whom you were sealed for the day of redemption. Get rid of all bitterness, rage and anger, brawling and slander, along with every form of malice. Be kind and compassionate to one another, forgiving each other, just as in Christ God forgave you.*

    EPHESIANS 4:28-32 (NIV)

2.  What does verse 28 teach us about the value and purpose of work?

    ------------------------------------------------------------

    ------------------------------------------------------------

    ------------------------------------------------------------

3. In verse 29, Paul commands us to "not let any unwholesome talk come out of our mouths." Read James 3:3-12 and from that passage write down three truths about the tongue.

_____

_____

_____

4. In verse 31, Paul lists six different words that describe sins of the heart and sins of the tongue. Do a little word study on these words to understand the different nuances of each word. If you don't have Bible language tools, you could look up these words in the dictionary.

## Do Life In Community

5. Get together with your spouse or a good friend and do a "language audit". Ask them to honestly assess your speech. Is it encouraging? Is it appropriate?

_____

_____

_____

**Be On Mission**

6.  What step of obedience or faith is God calling you to make based on this passage?

------------------------------------------------------------

------------------------------------------------------------

------------------------------------------------------------

Session 12

# The Power of Spiritual Training in the Transformation Process

## Part 2

**TRANS*formed***

The Miracle of Life Change

Take It In (Watch the video)

**Review from last session**

4.    Be Positive - Don't wound with your words.

> *Let no unwholesome word proceed from your mouth, but only*
> *such a word as is good for edification according to the need of the*
> *moment, so that it will give grace to those who hear. Do not grieve*
> *the Holy Spirit of God, by whom you were sealed for the day of*
> *redemption.*

EPHESIANS 4:29-30 (NASB)

**Spiritual Training Session #4**

O    **Training Objective:**

Positive Speech

O    **Train Command:**

"Say only what helps"

(the message of Ephesians 4:29)

O  **Training Actions**:

Put off – negative speech

Renew – recognize the power and consequences of your speech
Proverbs 18:21, Luke 6:45, Matthew 12:36-37

Put on – positive, encouraging speech

O  **Training Apparatus**:

Practice _____ and _____.

Memorize Ephesians 4:29

5.  _____ _____- Be the first to say "I'm sorry."

*Let all bitterness and wrath and anger and clamor and slander be
put away from you, along with all malice. Be kind to one another,
tender-hearted, forgiving each other, just as God in Christ also has
forgiven you*

EPHESIANS 4:31-32 (NASB)

**Spiritual Training Station #5**

O   **Training Objective:**

Relational Harmony

O   **Training Command:**

"Be kind, tender hearted, and forgiving"

(Ephesians 4:32)

O   **Training Actions:**

Put off – hate

Renew – remember that "right relationships" take precedent over my

"_____"

Put on – love

O   **Training Apparatus:**

The Matthew 5:24 Principle

**Summary:**

God has provided everything we need to live transformed, holy, and winsome lives. Our part is to appropriate His grace and power by going **into training** in the areas of:

○  Personal Integrity

○  Emotional Control

○  Financial Stewardship

○  Positive Speech

○  Private Attitudes

## Talk It Over

1.  When you think of these five habits that cultivate holiness, where have you seen progress? Is it in the area of being more honest, or in dealing with anger? Have you made progress in the area of being diligent, or being more positive with your words, or learning to genuinely forgive?

_____

_____

_____

2.  What is the one area where you need to go into training so you can experience transformation? What does "training" look like practically in that area?

    _____

    _____

    _____

3.  In this session, Chip talked about the practice of silence and solitude. How did that strike you? Is that something you long for? What would it look like to create space in your life for silence and solitude?

    _____

    _____

    _____

4.  Proverbs 10:19 (NASB) says, "When there are many words, transgression is unavoidable, but he who restrains his lips is wise."

    As you think about your life and relationships, where do you need to "restrain" your words? What are some practical methods or techniques you can use to do that?

    _____

    _____

    _____

## Live It Out – B.I.O.

The word "bio" means "life." Found in those three simple letters — B.I.O. — is the key to helping you become the person God wants you to be.

### B = COME "BEFORE GOD" DAILY

Meet with Him personally through prayer and His word to enjoy His presence, receive His direction, and follow His will.

### I = DO LIFE "IN COMMUNITY" WEEKLY

Structure your week to personally connect in safe relationships that provide love, support, transparency, challenge, and accountability.

### O = BE "ON MISSION" 24/7

Cultivate a mindset to live out Jesus' love for others through acts of sacrifice as well as service at home, work, play, and church.

**Come Before God**

5.   Colossians 3:13 (NIV) says:

*Bear with each other and forgive one another if any of you has a grievance against someone. Forgive as the Lord forgave you.*

Share about a time when you either received forgiveness from somebody else or extended forgiveness to someone.

### Do Life In Community

6.  Is there any relationship in your life where there is unresolved bitterness and anger? If there is, spend a little time as a group praying for that situation. Don't share details that would be inappropriate, but share the basic situation so that the group can know how to pray.

_____

_____

_____

### Be On Mission

7.  As you think about living the Christian life from this point forward, what is the single biggest takeaway from this series?

_____

_____

_____

## Accelerate (20 minutes that turn concepts into convictions)

**Inspiration** comes from hearing God's Word. **Motivation** grows by discussing God's Word. **Transformation** occurs when you study it for yourself.

If you want to "accelerate" your growth, here is an assignment you can do at home each week. Our convictions become even stronger when we dig into Scripture and discover truth for ourselves. To help you get the most out of this exercise, consider partnering up with someone in your group who will also commit to doing the assignment this week. Then, after you have each completed the assignment, agree to spend 10 minutes by phone sharing what you learned and what you are applying.

**Come Before God**

1.  Read the following passage slowly and carefully.

> *Then Peter came to Jesus and asked, "Lord, how many times shall I forgive my brother or sister who sins against me? Up to seven times?" Jesus answered, "I tell you, not seven times, but seventy-seven times. Therefore, the kingdom of heaven is like a king who wanted to settle accounts with his servants. As he began the settlement, a man who owed him ten thousand bags of gold was brought to him. Since he was not able to pay, the master ordered that he and his wife and his children and all that he had be sold to repay the debt. At this the servant fell on his knees before him. 'Be patient with me,' he begged, 'and I will pay back everything.' The servant's master took pity on him, canceled the debt and let him go. But when that servant went out, he found one of his fellow servants who owed him a hundred silver coins. He grabbed him and began to choke him. 'Pay back what you owe me!' he demanded. His fellow servant fell to his knees and begged him, 'Be patient with me, and I will pay it back.' But he refused. Instead, he went off and had the man thrown into prison until he could pay the debt. When the other servants saw what had happened, they were outraged and went and told their master everything that had happened. Then the master called the servant in. 'You wicked servant,' he said, 'I canceled all that debt of yours because you begged me to. Shouldn't you have had mercy on your fellow servant just as I had on you?' In anger his master handed him over to the jailers to be tortured, until he should pay back all he owed. This is how my heavenly Father will treat each of you unless you forgive your brother or sister from your heart.*

---

MATTHEW 18:21-35 (NIV)

2.  If you could summarize in one statement the teaching of Jesus in this parable, what would you say? Write out your answer.

    _____

    _____

    _____

3.  According to this story and the teaching of Ephesians 5:31-32, what is the basis of our forgiveness of others?

    _____

    _____

    _____

4.  Why do you think Jesus includes verse 34 and 35 and talks about the master handing over this wicked servant to the jailers to be tortured?

    _____

    _____

    _____

**Do Life In Community**

5. Who do you know that is living with a broken relationship and unresolved anger? Spend some time praying for that person and asking God to help them to forgive and restore the relationship.

**Be On Mission**

6. Matthew 5:23-24 (NIV) says:

*Therefore, if you are offering your gift at the altar and there remember that your brother or sister has something against you, leave your gift there in front of the altar. First go and be reconciled to them; then come and offer your gift.*

Is there anybody that you need to pursue to seek reconciliation and forgiveness? If so, take the steps outlined by Jesus here in Matthew 5.

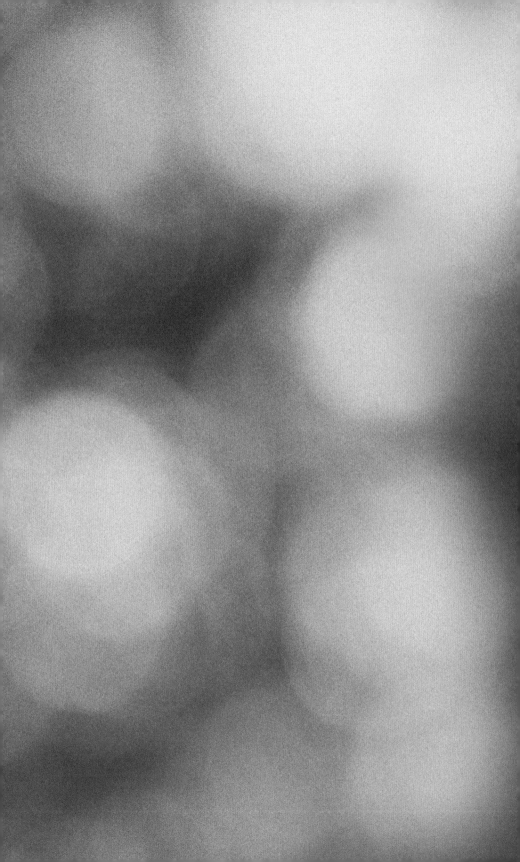

# Small Group
# Leader Resources

**TRANS*formed***
The Miracle of Life Change

## Group Agreement

People come to groups with a variety of expectations. The purpose of a group agreement is simply to make sure everyone is on the same page and that we have some common expectations.

The following Group Agreement is a tool to help you discuss specific guidelines during your first meeting. Modify anything that does not work for your group, then be sure to discuss the questions in the section called Our Game Plan. This will help you to have an even greater group experience!

We agree to the following priorities:

- Take the Bible Seriously – Seek to understand and apply God's truth in the Bible.

- Group Attendance – Give priority to the group meeting (call if I am going to be absent or late).

- Safe Environment – Create a safe place where people can be heard and feel loved (no snap judgments or simple fixes).

- Respectful Discussion – Speak in a respectful and honoring way to our mate and others in the group.

- Be Confidential – Keep anything that is shared strictly confidential and within the group.

- Spiritual Health – Give group members permission to help me live a godly, healthy spiritual life that is pleasing to God.

- Building Relationships – Get to know the other members of the group and pray for them regularly.

- Pursue B.I.O. – Encourage and challenge each other in coming "Before God," doing life together "In Community" and being "On Mission 24/7."

- Prayer – Regularly pray with and for each other.

- Other

Our game plan:

1.  What day and time will we meet?

    _____

    _____

    _____

2.  Where will we meet?

    _____

    _____

    _____

3.  How long will we meet each week?

    _____

    _____

    _____

4.  What will we do for refreshments?

    _____

    _____

    _____

5.  What will we do about childcare?

    _____

    _____

    _____

## Leader Notes

As an additional resource to help you in leading your group, we have prepared brief coaching videos. These 3-minute videos can be found online at livingontheedge.org/group-studies/free-group-leader-course/.

## How to Make This a Meaningful Group Experience

Before the group arrives

1.  Be prepared. Your personal preparation can make a huge difference in the quality of the group experience. We strongly suggest previewing both the DVD teaching by Chip Ingram and the study guide.

2.  Pray for your group members by name. Ask God to use your time together to touch the heart of every person in your group. Expect God to challenge and change people as a result of this study.

3.  Provide refreshments. There's nothing like food to help a group relax and connect with each other. For the first week, we suggest you prepare a snack, but after that, ask other group members to bring the food so that they share in the responsibilities of the group and make a commitment to return.

4.  Relax. Don't try to imitate someone else's style of leading a group. Lead the group in a way that fits your style and temperament. Remember that people may feel nervous showing up for a small group study, so put them at ease when they arrive. Make sure to have all the details covered prior to your group meeting, so that once people start arriving, you can focus on them.

## Take It In

1.  Get the video ready. Each video session will have 3 components. The first couple of minutes Chip will introduce this week's topic Then, you will watch the actual teaching content that Chip taught in front of a live audience. This portion of the video will be roughly 25 minutes in length. Finally, Chip will then share some closing thoughts and set up the discussion time for your group.

2. **Have ample materials.** Before you start the video, make sure everyone has their own copy of the study guide. Encourage the group to follow along in their study guides, as the outline provides an opportunity to fill in the blanks and take notes.

3. **Arrange the room.** Set up the chairs in the room so that everyone can see the television. Arrange the room in such a way that it is conducive to discussion.

## Talk It Over

Here are some guidelines for leading the discussion time:

1. **Make this a discussion, not a lecture.** Resist the temptation to do all the talking, and to answer your own questions. Don't be afraid of a few moments of silence while people formulate their answers.

   Don't feel like you need to have all the answers. There is nothing wrong with simply saying, "I don't know the answer to that, but I'll see if I can find an answer this week."

2. **Encourage everyone to participate.** Don't let one person dominate, but also don't pressure quieter members to speak during the first couple of sessions. Be patient. Ask good follow up questions and be sensitive to delicate issues.

3. **Affirm people's participation and input.** If an answer is clearly wrong, ask "What led you to that conclusion?" or ask what the rest of the group thinks. If a disagreement arises, don't be too quick to shut it down! The discussion can draw out important perspectives, and if you can't resolve it there, offer to research it further and return to the issue next week.

   However, if someone goes on the offensive and engages in personal attack, you will need to step in as the leader. In the midst of spirited discussion, we must also remember that people are fragile and there is no place for disrespect.

4. **Detour when necessary.** If an important question is raised that is not in the study guide, take time to discuss it. Also, if someone shares something personal and emotional, take time for them. Stop and pray for them right then. Allow the Holy Spirit room to maneuver, and follow His prompting when the discussion changes direction.

5. Subgroup. One of the principles of small group life is "when numbers go up, sharing goes down." So, if you have a large group, sometimes you may want to split up into groups of 4-6 for the discussion time. This is a great way to give everyone, even the quieter members, a chance to share. Choose someone in the group to guide each of the smaller groups through the discussion. This involves others in the leadership of the group, and provides an opportunity for training new leaders.

6. Prayer. Be sensitive to the fact that some people in your group may be uncomfortable praying out loud. As a general rule, don't call on people to pray unless you have asked them ahead of time or have heard them pray in public. But this can also be a time to help people build their confidence to pray in a group. Consider having prayer times that ask people to just say a word or sentence of thanks to God.

## Live It Out — B.I.O.

BIO is a word that is synonymous with "life". The key to helping you become the person God wants you to be is found in these three simple letters: B.I.O.

### B = Come "Before God" daily

Meet with Him personally through His word and prayer to enjoy His presence, receive His direction, and follow His will.

### I = Do Life "In Community" weekly

Structure your week to personally connect in safe relationships that provide love, support, transparency, challenge, and accountability.

### O = Be "On Mission" 24/7

Cultivate a mindset to "live out" Jesus' love for others through acts of sacrifice and service at home, work, play, and church

## Accelerate (20 minutes that turn concepts into convictions)

Inspiration comes from hearing God's Word; motivation grows by discussing God's Word; transformation occurs when you study it for yourself.

If you want to "accelerate" your growth, here is an assignment you can do this week. To help you get the most out of this exercise, consider partnering up with somebody in your group who will also commit to do the assignment this week. Then, after you have each done the assignment, agree to spend 10 minutes by phone to share what you learned and what you are applying.

## Session Notes

Thanks for hosting this series on spiritual transformation. This practical series will help you discover how you can partner with God to experience the abundant life He has for you. Whether you are brand new at leading a small group or you are a seasoned veteran, God is going to use you. God has a long history of using ordinary people to get his work done.

These brief notes are intended to help prepare you for each week's session. By spending just a few minutes each week previewing the video and going over these session notes, you will set the table for a great group experience. Also, don't forget to pray for your group each week.

### Session 1 — Is a "Changed Life" Really Possible?, Pt. 1

- If your group doesn't know each other well, be sure that you spend some time getting acquainted. Don't rush right into the video lesson. Remember, small groups are not just about a study or a meeting, they are about relationships.

- Be sure to capture everyone's contact information. It is a good idea to send out an e-mail with everybody's contact information so that the group can stay in touch. At the back of your study guide is a roster where people can fill in the names and contact information of the other group members.

- When you are ready to start the session, be sure that each person in your group has a copy of the study guide. The small group study guide is important for people to follow along and to take notes.

- Spend a little time in this first session talking about B.I.O. These three core practices are the pathway to maturity. You will see these letters and terms throughout this curriculum. Start getting your group comfortable with the concepts of "coming before God", "doing life together in community", and "being on mission."

- Facilitating the discussion time. Sometimes Chip will ask you as the facilitator to lead the way by answering the first question. This allows you to lead by example and your willingness to share openly about your life will help others feel the permission to do the same.

- Before you wrap up your group time, be sure to introduce the Accelerate exercise in the study guide. This is an assignment they can do during the week that will help turbo charge their growth as a parent. Encourage them to find a partner in the group who they can talk to each week about the accelerate exercise.

- It would be a good idea to review the discussion questions for this week's session. There are a total of 7 discussion questions each week. If that is too many for your group to get through, you might want to decide ahead of time which questions you want your group to discuss.

- In this week's session question #2 asks "what's one thing you would really like for God to change in your life?" This could be an intimidating question to some in your group. So, it might be best for you as the leader to be the first to share your answer to this question.

## Session 2 — Is a "Changed Life" Really Possible? (Part 2)

- Why not begin your preparation by praying right now for the people in your group? You might even want to keep their names in your Bible. You may also want to ask people in your group how you can pray for them specifically.

- If somebody doesn't come back this week, be sure and follow up with them. Even if you knew they were going to have to miss the group meeting, give them a call or shoot them an e-mail letting them know that they were missed. It would also be appropriate to have a couple of other people in the group let them know they were missed.

- If you haven't already previewed the video, take the time to do so. It will help you know how to best facilitate the group and what are the best discussion questions for your group.

- During the early part of this session, Chip will talk about performance-based (rules-based) Christianity. A lot of Christians grew up under the bondage and guilt of legalism. It is crucial that your group understand the difference between a performance-based and grace-based view of the Christian life.

- One of the discussion questions this week asks people how they are doing at consistently coming before God and spending time in Scripture. It is likely that some in your group struggle with this. Let people know that this struggle is very common for believers. The goal of the question is not to invoke guilt. The goal is to spark a discussion that might help people in your group take steps to consistently be in God's Word.

## Session 3 — Where Do We Get the Power to Change? (Part 1)

- Did anybody miss last week's session? If so, make it a priority to follow up and let them know they were missed. It just might be your care for them that keeps them connected to the group.

- Share the load. One of the ways to raise the sense of ownership within the group is to get them involved in more than coming to the meeting. So, get someone to help with refreshments… find somebody else to be in charge of the prayer requests… get someone else to be in charge of any social gathering you plan… let someone else lead the discussion one night. Give away as much of the responsibility as possible. That is GOOD leadership.

- Think about last week's meeting for a moment. Was there anyone that didn't talk or participate? In every group, there are extroverts and there are introverts. There are people who like to talk and then there are those who are quite content NOT to talk. Not everyone engages in the same way or at the same level but you do want to try and create an environment where everyone wants to participate.

- Follow up with your group this week to see how they did with the Accelerate assignment this week. Don't shame or embarrass anyone who didn't get to the assignment, but honestly challenge them to make this a priority in the coming week.

- As you begin your session this week you might to check in with your group members to see how they did in spending time in God's Word this past week.

- The passage Chip will teach from this week (Ephesians 4:7-10) is a challenging and difficult passage of Scripture to understand. Make sure the group focuses on the big idea that the death of Jesus on the cross is key to our victory over sin.

## Session 4 — Where Do We Get the Power to Change? (Part 2)

- Don't feel any pressure to get through all the questions. As people open up and talk, don't move on too quickly. Give them the space to consider what is going on inside them as they interact with this teaching.

- Don't be afraid of silence. When you ask people a question, give them time to think about it. Don't feel like you have to fill every quiet moment with words.

- If your group is not sharing as much as you would like or if the discussion is being dominated by a person or two, try subgrouping. If your group is 8 people or more, this is a great way to up the level of participation.

  After watching the video teaching, you could divide the group into a couple of smaller groups for the discussion time. It is good to get someone you think would be a good facilitator to agree to this ahead of time.

- The opening discussion question this week asks people to share what they believe is their spiritual gift. If they have never been through any kind of gifts assessment, just have them share what they think they are good at.

- Discussion question #6 this week will address the issue of "identity". This is an area where a lot of people struggle. You might want to share with the group your own journey with learning to find your identity in Christ rather than in success, wealth, or people pleasing.

## Session 5 — How to Become the Person You've Always Longed to Be (Part 1)

- Confidentiality is crucial to group life. The moment trust is breached, people will shut down and close up. So, you may want to mention the importance of confidentiality again this week just to keep it on people's radar.

- Each time your group meets, take a few minutes to update on what has happened since the last group meeting. Ask people what they are learning and putting into practice. Remember, being a disciple of Jesus means becoming a "doer of the word."

- As you begin this week's session, it would be a good idea to check in with the group regarding the Accelerate exercise that they have been challenged to do as homework. If people are doing the exercise, ask them what they have been learning and how it impacting them. If they haven't been doing the exercise, encourage them to commit to it this next week.

- In discussion question #2 this week, your group will be asked to assess the equipping mindset in their church. Be sure not to let the discussion drift into blaming or fault-finding with the church.

- The last discussion question this week challenges your group members to start investing in others. Many Christians feel inadequate or unqualified to equip or invest in someone else. Help them see that they DO have something to offer and that their greatest "ability" is their "availability".

## Session 6 — How to Become the Person You've Always Longed to Be (Part 2)

- You are now at the halfway point of this series. How is it going? How well is the group connecting? What has been going well and what needs a little work? Are there any adjustments you need to make?

- One way to deepen the level of community within your group is to spend time together outside the group meeting. If you have not already done so, plan something that will allow you to get to know each other better. Also, consider having someone else in the group take responsibility for your fellowship event.

- As you begin this week's session, do a check-in to see what people are learning and applying from this series. Don't be afraid to take some time at the beginning of your meeting to review some key ideas from the previous week's lessons.

- The opening discussion question will ask the group to take the Diagnostic Evaluation. You might want to print off a couple of copies from your study guide just in case people show up without their book.

- Be sure to have some fun with discussion question #3 this week. Your group will be asked "If time and money were no limitation, what kind of ministry would you dream of being involved in?" Challenge the group to really dream and think outside the box. This could be a very important defining moment in somebody's life.

## Session 7 — How to "Break Out" of a Destructive Lifestyle (Part 1)

- Consider asking someone in your group to facilitate next week's lesson. Who knows, there might be a great potential small group leader in your group. It will give you a break and give them a chance to grow.

- Consider sending an e-mail to each person in your group this week letting them know you prayed for them today. Also, let them know that you are grateful that they are in the group.

- Take a few minutes this week before you get into the study to talk about the impact of this series so far. Ask people what they are learning, applying, and changing in their lives. For this series to have lasting impact it has to be more than just absorbing information. So, challenge your group to put what they are learning into action.

- Revisit the importance of B.I.O. this week. Reinforce the importance of people integrating these core practices in their lives. For example, talk about the priority of coming before God each day and submitting to the authority of God's truth.

- The opening discussion question asks people to define the phrase "Christian lifestyle". We all bring our assumptions and presuppositions to our view of the Christian life. But ask people if their definition really fits with the teaching of Scripture.

- Then, you will be asked to divide the group up by men and women for the rest of the discussion time. Because of the sensitive nature of this week's discussion about moral purity, it will be best to have the men and women have separate discussions. It would be good ahead of time to ask someone to facilitate the group (men or women) that you won't be leading.

## Session 8 — How to "Break Out" of a Destructive Lifestyle (Part 2)

- In your group meetings, be sure to take adequate time for prayer. Don't just tack it on at the end of the meeting simply out of obligation. Also, don't be afraid to stop the meeting and pray for someone who shares a need or a struggle.

- The 2nd discussion question this week will ask people in your group what habit, behavior, or attitude they need to "put off". This could be an intimidating question, so it might be helpful for you as the leader to take the lead in sharing honestly from your own life.

- As part of this week's discussion, your group will be challenged to memorize a passage of Scripture together. You could select any passage that seems fitting for your group, but the suggestion is given of memorizing Romans 12:1-2. Encourage the group to take this seriously and then commit to check in with each other during the week.

## Session 9 — The Role of "Spiritual Training" in the Transformation Process (Part 1)

- This week, Chip is going to start talking about five habits that cultivate holiness in our lives. The first one has to do with honesty. You might consider sharing some subtle ways that we can be dishonest. It might be easy for the group to focus on blatant lies rather than on the subtle, more socially acceptable ways we are dishonest.

- Question five this week has to do with confession and is based on James 5:16. Confession is something we don't talk about much in the church these days, but this passage is clear about the power of honest confession.

- This week's Accelerate exercise is based on Psalm 15, a great passage about integrity. Encourage and challenge your group to spend the 20 minutes doing the Accelerate assignment sometime this week.

## Session 10 — The Role of "Spiritual Training" in the Transformation Process (Part 2)

- Don't forget to celebrate what God has been teaching you and doing in the lives of group members. You might want to take some time at the beginning of this week's session to have people share how this series has impacted them.

- Do a brief check in as you start this session to see how people did at being more honest this past week. We are not looking for perfection, but progress. Keep bringing people back to the word picture of going into training.

- During this session, Chip will continue to talk about the five habits that cultivate holiness. It would be good for you to remind the group about honesty, the first habit Chip taught on during the last session. And, that is the habit of honesty.

- The focus of this session will be anger. Straight out of Ephesians 4, Chip will help us see righteous anger and also unrighteous anger. He will also provide some very clear and practical techniques that can help us deal with anger.

## Session 11 — The Power of "Spiritual Training" in the Transformation Process (Part 1)

- Since this is the next to the last week of this study, you might want to spend some time this week talking about what your group is going to do after your complete this study.

- As this series winds down, this is a good time to plan some kind of party or fellowship after you complete the study. Find the "party person" in your group and ask them to take on the responsibility of planning a fun experience for the group. Also, use this party as a time for people to share how God has used this series to grow them and change them.

- It would be good this week to review the first two habits of cultivating holiness that Chip has already covered: honesty and anger.

- One of the things Chip will teach on and encourage this week is the creation of a "to be" list. Really challenge people to work on developing this in the coming days.

- In this session, Chip will also talk a lot about the power of our words. As the leader of your group, you might want to consider speaking words of affirmation and blessing to those in your group.

## Session 12 — The Power of "Spiritual Training" in the Transformation Process (Part 2)

- Be sure that everyone is clear what your group is doing next after this study.

- Once again, spend a few minutes reviewing the four habits that Chip has already covered. Those are the habits of being honest, being angry, being diligent, and being positive with your words.

- During this session, Chip will talk about the practices of silence and solitude. These practices can feel foreign in our busy and fast-paced world. Encourage the group to set aside some time this next week to be quiet and just "be with God".

- The majority of this session will focus on the issue of forgiveness. This could potentially be a painful topic for a person or two in your group. So, come to this session prayed up. Question six will ask people if there is any relationship in their life where there is unresolved bitterness and anger. If someone does share about a broken relationship, be sure to take the time to listen, care, and pray for them. This is the time to practice the "ministry of presence" and just be there to support your group member.

## Prayer and Praise

One of the most important things you can do in your group is to pray with and for each other. Write down each other's concerns here so you can remember to pray for these requests during the week!

Use the Follow Up box to record an answer to a prayer or to write down how you might want to follow up with the person making the request. This could be a phone call, an e-mail or a card. Your personal concern will mean a lot!

| Date | Person | Prayer Request | Follow Up |
|------|--------|----------------|-----------|
|      |        |                |           |
|      |        |                |           |
|      |        |                |           |
|      |        |                |           |
|      |        |                |           |

| Date | Person | Prayer Request | Follow Up |
|------|--------|----------------|-----------|
|      |        |                |           |
|      |        |                |           |
|      |        |                |           |
|      |        |                |           |
|      |        |                |           |
|      |        |                |           |
|      |        |                |           |

| Date | Person | Prayer Request | Follow Up |
|------|--------|----------------|-----------|
|      |        |                |           |
|      |        |                |           |
|      |        |                |           |
|      |        |                |           |
|      |        |                |           |
|      |        |                |           |
|      |        |                |           |

| Date | Person | Prayer Request | Follow Up |
|------|--------|----------------|-----------|
|      |        |                |           |
|      |        |                |           |
|      |        |                |           |
|      |        |                |           |
|      |        |                |           |
|      |        |                |           |
|      |        |                |           |

| Date | Person | Prayer Request | Follow Up |
|------|--------|----------------|-----------|
|      |        |                |           |
|      |        |                |           |
|      |        |                |           |
|      |        |                |           |
|      |        |                |           |
|      |        |                |           |
|      |        |                |           |

| Date | Person | Prayer Request | Follow Up |
|------|--------|----------------|-----------|
|      |        |                |           |
|      |        |                |           |
|      |        |                |           |
|      |        |                |           |
|      |        |                |           |
|      |        |                |           |
|      |        |                |           |

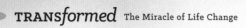

| Date | Person | Prayer Request | Follow Up |
|------|--------|----------------|-----------|
|      |        |                |           |
|      |        |                |           |
|      |        |                |           |
|      |        |                |           |
|      |        |                |           |
|      |        |                |           |
|      |        |                |           |

| Date | Person | Prayer Request | Follow Up |
| --- | --- | --- | --- |
|  |  |  |  |
|  |  |  |  |
|  |  |  |  |
|  |  |  |  |
|  |  |  |  |
|  |  |  |  |
|  |  |  |  |

## Group Roster

| Name | Home Phone | Email |
|------|-----------|-------|
|      |           |       |
|      |           |       |
|      |           |       |
|      |           |       |
|      |           |       |
|      |           |       |
|      |           |       |
|      |           |       |
|      |           |       |
|      |           |       |
|      |           |       |
|      |           |       |
|      |           |       |

# What's Next?
More Group Studies from Chip Ingram:

## Balancing Life's Demands
Biblical Priorities for a Busy Life
Busy, tired and stressed out? Learn how to put "first things first" and find peace in the midst of pressure and adversity.

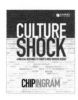

## Culture Shock
A Biblical Response to Today's Most Divisive Issues
Bring light—not heat—to divisive issues, such as abortion, homosexuality, sex, politics, the environment, politics and more.

## Doing Good
What Happens When Christians Really Live Like Christians
This series clarifies what Doing Good will do in you and then through you, for the benefit of others and the glory of God.

## Experiencing God's Dream for Your Marriage
Practical Tools for a Thriving Marriage
Examine God's design for marriage and the real life tools and practices that will transform it for a lifetime.

## Five Lies that Ruin Relationships
Building Truth-Based Relationships
Uncover five powerful lies that wreck relationships and experience the freedom of understanding how to recognize God's truth.

## The Genius of Generosity
Lessons from a Secret Pact Between Friends
The smartest financial move you can make is to invest in God's Kingdom. Learn His design for wise giving and generous living.

*Watch previews and order at livingontheedge.org.*

## The Real God
### How He Longs for You to See Him
A deeper look at seven attributes of God's character that will change the way you think, pray and live.

## Good to Great in God's Eyes
### 10 Practices Great Christians Have in Common
If you long for spiritual breakthrough, take a closer look at ten powerful practices that will rekindle a fresh infusion of faith.

## The Real Heaven
### It's Not What You Think
Chip Ingram digs into scripture to reveal what heaven will be like, what we'll do there, and how we're to prepare for eternity today.

## Holy Ambition
### Turning God-Shaped Dreams Into Reality
Do you long to turn a God-inspired dream into reality? Learn how God uses everyday believers to accomplish extraordinary things.

## House or Home: Marriage Edition
### God's Blueprint for a Great Marriage
Get back to the blueprint and examine God's plan for marriages that last for a lifetime.

## House or Home: Parenting Edition
### God's Blueprint for Biblical Parenting
Timeless truths about God's blueprint for parenting, and the potential to forever change the trajectory of your family.

*Watch previews and order at livingontheedge.org.*

## What's Next?
More Group Studies from Chip Ingram:

### The Invisible War
The Believer's Guide to Satan, Demons and Spiritual Warfare
Learn how to clothe yourself with God's "spiritual armor" and be confident of victory over the enemy of your soul.

### Love, Sex and Lasting Relationships  `UPDATED`
God's Prescription to Enhance Your Love Life
Do you believe in "true love"? Discover a better way to find love, stay in love, and build intimacy that lasts a lifetime.

### Overcoming Emotions that Destroy
Constructive Tools for Destructive Emotions
We all struggle with destructive emotions that can ruin relationships. Learn God's plan to overcome angry feelings for good.

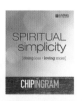

### Spiritual Simplicity
Doing Less · Loving More
If you crave simplicity and yearn for peace this study is for you. Spiritual simplicity can only occur when we do less and love more.

### Transformed
The Miracle of Life Change
Ready to make a change? Explore God's process of true transformation and learn to spot barriers that hold you back from receiving God's best.

### True Spirituality
Becoming a Romans 12 Christian
We live in a world that is activity-heavy and relationship-light. Learn the next steps toward True Spirituality.

*Watch previews and order at livingontheedge.org.*

## What's Next?

More Group Studies from Chip Ingram:

### Why I Believe

Answers to Life's Most Difficult Questions

Can miracles be explained? Is there really a God? There are solid, logical answers about claims of the Christian faith.

### Your Divine Design

Discover, Develop and Deploy Your Spiritual Gifts

How has God uniquely wired you? Discover God's purpose for spiritual gifts and how to identify your own.

## Download the Chip Ingram App

The Chip Ingram App delivers daily devotionals, broadcasts, message notes, blog articles and more right on your mobile device.